HORACE IN ENGLISH LITERATURE

by

CORA DAVIS SMITH

A Thesis Submitted for the Degree of

MASTER OF ARTS

UNIVERSITY OF WISCONSIN

1917

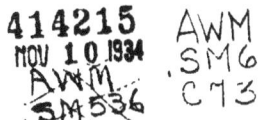
It will be quite impossible, within the scope of this
thesis, to make a complete and exhaustive study of the influence
of Horace on English Literature.   But, by citing a number of
quotations from the best known writers, we shall attempt to
show how universal has been his influence, from Chaucer to
Browning.   Among these quotations, we shall use direct refer-
ences to Horace, his life or works; quotations from and obvious
translations or imitations of his works; and finally passages
containing that intangible quality which we call the spirit
of Horace.

We shall try not to be guilty of the charge with which
Tennyson accused his critics: that he could not even mention
"the moaning of the sea" or the "crests of the waves" without
being charged with plagiarism.   Only such passages as are of
obviously Horatian influence will be quoted.

I am especially indebted for my material to Eward
Stemplinger, "Das Fortleben der Horazichen Lyrik seit der Ren-
aissance;" Dr. Hugo Reinsch, "Jonson's Beziehungen zu Horaz;"
W.P.Mustard, "Classical Echoes in Tennyson;" Mary Rebecca
Thayer, "The Influence of Horace on the Chief Poets of the 19th
Century;" and various works of criticism of the works of the
poets whom I shall consider.

In all ages, among all nations, Horace has ever been a
general favorite.   Very early, his works were used as text books
by the boys in the schools at Rome, and today in Germany, France,
England and America, we still are studying the poems of Horace.
Even in the Middle Ages when Classical Literature, especially
that which favored of paganism, had a hard struggle for existence,
Horace was preserved.   The fact that there are two hundred and
fifty extant manuscripts is sufficient proof of that statement.
In this connection we naturally think of Sophocles, Euripides
and Aeschylus, the greater part of whose plays have been entire-
ly lost; of Lucilius of whose works we have practically nothing;
of the lost volumes of Livy; of the wretched manuscripts of
Plautus and Terence; of Catullus, Tibullus and Propertius.
All these bear witness to the evident popularity which saved
Horace from at least partial oblivion with the others.

In the Middle Ages, Horace was better known for his
didactic than for his lyric works.[1]   Eward Moore in his book
"Studies in Dante", gives a table which shows this fact very
clearly.   I shall quote here, only the part which has to do
with English literature.

Cent.	Odes & Epodes	Sat.& Epist.
VIII	48	72
IX - X	55	19
XI	54	127
XII	77	520
XIII	16	299

---

1. Edward Moore - "Studies in Dante", p. 201.

[1]
Manilius explains the evident falling off in the
thirteenth century by the effect of the Crusades.   But the fact
that Horace was very well known, on the Continent as well as in
England is clearly evidenced by the fact that Dante selects him
as one of the five great poets of antiquity.   Inferno, 4. 89.

[2]
Stemplinger gives the date of the first full transla-
tion of Horace works as 1625 by Thomas Hawkins.   Long before
this, there had been translations of various forms.   In 1566,
Thomas Drant had published "A Medicinable Morall, that is,
The Two Books of Horace, his Satyres Englyshed according to the
prescriptions of St.Hierome."   Warton and Henry Howard were
also early translators.   During this early period, the trans-
lations followed the text very closely, and the style was liable
to be stiff and formal. There was a tendency too in this era,
extending over into the one following, to nationalize, or to
fit to English setting the poems of Horace.   Thus in 1692
Prior imitates O. III, 2 as a lament for slothful England.
Milton, "What the Swed intend and what the French."
O. II, 11, 1. "Quid bellicosus Cantaber."

---

1. Manilius, "Horace and Dante."

2. Stemplinger, "Das Fortleben der Horazischen Lyrik seit der
        Renaissance."

Later Pope adapts the names of English poets to Horace
O. IV, 9.

>"Non, si priores Maeonius tenet
>sedes Homerus, Pindaricae latent
>   Ceaeque et Alcaei minaces
>   Stesichorique graves camenae,
>nec, si quid olim Iusit Anacreon."

>"Tho daring Milton sits sublime
>In Spenser Native Muses play
>Nor yet shall Waller yield to time
>Nor pensive Cowley's moral lay."

In Allan Ramsay, Soracte becomes "Pentland's towering
gap."

Horace walking in the wood when a wolf flees from him,
O. I, 22 is paralleled by Hughes walking in St.James Park in
London.

The best known translators of this early period are
Drant, Ahsmore, Ben Jonson, Sir John Beaumont, Sir Thomas Haw-
kins, Sir Richard Faushawe, and Barton Holyday.

In 1665 Milton translated Ode I, 5,

>"Quis multa gracilis te puer in rosa."

This has been called the high water mark of Translation and

marked the beginning of a new era.   From this time until
1800 the translations were very smooth and harmonious with a
tendency toward freedom and imitation.   Horace was the inspir-
ation, the model, of poets of this age.   Everyone translated
or imitated his works.   Lord Lytton says that,"From the middle
of the 17th century there is scarcely a man of letters who has
not at one time or other translated or imitated some of the
odes." The best known are Dryden, Addison, Swift, Pope, Ben
Jonson, Cowper and Warren Hastings.   Sainte Beuve classes
"the tendency to translate Horace with the lesser ailments
that youthful flesh is heir to."[1]   R.G.Tucker expressed a
similar thot, "Time was and not so long ago, when Horace was
more read and quoted than any other poet of antiquity.   He
was quoted at dinners, in literature, in Parliament.   It was
taken for granted that he represented the ne plus ultra of lyric
quality.

"Upon English Literature the Latin lyrists and more
especially Horace, have exercised a far-reaching influence,
sometimes with the full consciousness of the English poet, more
often indirectly.   The "Horatian Ode", that is to say, the
ode in which there is but one comparative short form of stanza
repeated throughout, explains its own genesis by its name.

----

1. R.G.Tucker, "Foreign Debt to English Literature."

In other cases of English lyrics it is not easy, nor is it
necessary to distinguish precisely between the debt due to the
Latin writers and that due to native grown song and ballad.
English lyrics of feeling would necessarily have developed
themselves in some shape without the aid of foreign example,.
but in point of fact, the Elizabethans, and still more the
cavalier poets of the seventeenth century were in the habit
of looking to Horace, and in a less degree to Catullus, for
suggestions of form and expression, and occasionally of thought.
For one external indication of this attitude, we may look to
the practice of the school of Herrick, Suckling, Lovelace and
Waller, who (following the Elizabethan sonneteers) habitually
call their inspiring mistresses by the names of "Lesbia",
"Delia", "Chloe" and the like for no other reason than that
these are the non-committal names sanctioned by the usage of
the Latin lyrists.

From 1800 down to the present time there have been fewer
translations,- Newman, Ravensworth, Lytton, Martin, Conington,
Thornton, Rutherford, Clark, DeVere, and Gladstone are the
names most worthy of note,- but later I shall show that while
the great poets of this era were not slavish imitators, still
the influence of Horace can be clearly traced in their works.

———————

1
Geoffrey Chaucer, 1328-1400.

In Chaucer, we have only about three references to
Horace and all of these are from the Epistles.   As I pointed
out above, the lyric poems were little known at this period,
while the didactic works were more widely read.   However, it
is very evident that Chaucer did not know Horace,- had probably
never seen his works in complete form if at all.

A.P.70-73. "Multa renascentur quae iam cecidere, cadentque
Quae nunc sunt in honore vocabula, si volet unus,
Quem penes arbitrium est et ius et norma loquendi."

Troil II, 22.

"Ye knoweek, that in forme of speche in chaunge
Withinne a thousand yeer, and words though
That hydden prys, now wonder nyce and straunge
We thinketh them."

A.P.1-4   "Humano capiti cervicem pictor equinam
Iungam si velit et varias inducere plumas
Undique conlatis membris, ut turpiter atrum
Desinat in piscem mulier formosa superne:"

Troil I, 1041.

"For if a peyntom wolde peynite a pyk
With asses feet and hede it asanape,
It cordeth nought."

---

1. Skeat's edition of Chaucer - Introduction.

Troil I, 394.

"As writ myn autour called hollius."

It is unknown why Chaucer used the name of "hollius" here, for the passage which follows is an imitation from Petrarch.[1] Dr. Latham has suggested that Chaucer misread the line in Horace Ep. I, 21. "Troiani belli scriptorem, maxime holli," and thence derived the notion that hollius wrote in the Trojan war. This becomes more likely if we suppose that he merely saw the line quoted apart from the context. This seems not only possible but quite probable when we remember that medieval writers obtained much of their information from manuscript notebooks which contained hundreds of choice passages from all sorts of authors, collected by diligent compilers.

From the context we see that hollius is to Chaucer a mere name which he used in his usual manner of convenient embellishment, as in other places he mentions Homer, Dares, and Dictys, tho he probably knew next to nothing of any of them.

---

1. Works of Chaucer - Skeat, Vol. II, LIII, 464, and Vol. III, 277.

Edmund Spenser - 1552-1599.

Spenser evidently was very familiar with Horace, for thro'out "Fairy Queen" he has scattered passages which are practically translations.

Ep. II, 1, 143-4.

"Piabant

Floribus et vino Genium memorem brevis aevi."

F.22 Str. 49.

With diverse flowers he daintily was deckt

And strowed around about and by his side,

A mighty mazer bowl of wine was sett

As if it had to him been sacrifide.

Odes I, 23, 1-8.

"Vitas inuleo me similis, Chloe,

quaerenti pavidam montibus aviis

matrem non sine vano

aurarum et siluae metu."

"Nam seu mobilibus veris inhorruit

adventus foliis, seu virides rubum

dimovere lacertae,

et corde et genibus tremit."

———————

Faery Qu. III, 7, 1, 1-5.

> "Like as a hynde forth singled from the herd
> That hath escaped from a ravenous beaste
> Yet flies away of her own feet afearde
> And every leaf that shaketh with the least
> Murmur of wind, her terror hath increased.

1.
William Shakespeare 1564-1616.

Shakespeare was probably not very well versed in Horace, H.R.D. Anders tells us that Shakespeare mentions Horace only twice in his plays and those times, not showing a very great knowledge of him.

Titus Andronicus IV, 2, 20-3. Demetrius quotes "Integer vitae scelerisque purus." Chiron answers, "Oh! tis a verse in Horace, I know it well, I read it in a grammar long ago." The reference is to Lily's grammar which was filled with Latin quotations. Shakespeare often refers to it, and had probably studied it as a boy in school.

Love's Labour Lost IV, 2, 95. Holofernes: "As Horace says in his" Here he interrupts himself and does not make any quotation.

From these references we conclude that Shakespeare had heard of Horace, but probably had never studied his works.

---

1. H.R.D.Anders, "Shakespeare's Books."

Ben Jonson, 1574-1637.

Stemplinger tells us that Ben Jonson made more use of Horace than any other poet. "He interweaves quotations in his works or puts them into the mouths of his dramatic characters. He translates Horace, imitates him, and delights his learned readers with countless Horatian allusions."[1] Dr. Hugo Reinsch says that Jonson was the most influenced of English writers. "He quotes Headley "Were the ancients to claim their property, Jonson would not have a rag to cover his nakedness."

He frequently mentions Horace's personal appearance. Poetaster IV, 511.

"Juppiter save thee, my good poet, my noble prophet, my little fat Horace."

Elegy VII, 411. "Let me be what I am, as Virgil cold, as Horace fat, or as Anacreon, old.

He also refers to him as a poet.

Masque of Queens VII, 117 "The best artist."

"   " Augurs VII, 439 "Doctissima poeta."

"   " Oberon VII, 183 "The wise Horace."

Ode to Himself, VII, 202. "Fit to be

Sung by a Horace, or a muse as free."

Inviting a friend to supper -

---

1. Muncheuer, Beitrage zur romanischen und Englischen Philologie. Thesis - "Jonson's Beziehungen zu Horaz." Hugo Reinsch.

"A pure cup of rich canary wine

Of which had Horace or Anacreon tasted,

Their lives as do their lines, till now had lasted."

He often puts quotations into the mouths of his characters.

Prologue - "Every man out of his Humour". "As Horace
says, Mean cates are welcome still to hungry guests."

Sat. II, 2-38.

"Ieiunus raro stomachus volgaria temnit."

Hue and Cry after Cupid.

"Sports and pretty lightnesses that a company

have under the Titles of Joci and Risus; and are

said to accompany Venus."

cp. Odes I, 2, 33-4.

"Erycina ridens,

Quam Iocus circumvolat et Cupido."

Mottoes for his dramas are frequently quotations.

Every Man out of His Humour.

"Non aliena meo pressi pede se proprius stes

Te capiunt magis - et decies repetita placebunt."

cp. A.P. 301-5.

"Every Man -"

"Oh, he's a black fellow, take heed of him."

Sat. I, 4, 85.

"Hic niger est, hunc tu Romane caveto."

———

"Every Man - "

> "Poor worms, they hiss at me, whilst I at home
> Can be content to applaud myself."

Sat. 1, 66.

> "Populus mihi sibilat, at mihi plaudo
> ipse domi."

As Stemplinger says, Jonson translated and imitated Horace very extensively.   Swinburne expresses his opinion of Jonson's translations in no uncertain terms.   "A worse translator than Ben Jonson never committed a double outrage on two languages at once ---- The translation (of Ars Poetica) is one of those miracles of incompetence, incongruity, and insensibility, which must be seen to be believed."[1]

While Jonson's translations are not as impossible as Swinburne would have us believe, they are not equal to the later school of Pope and his contemporaries.   Some of them however are very good.   Take for example A.P. 4-10.

> "Pictoribus atque poetis
> Quidlibet audendi semper fuit aequa potestas
> Scimus."
> But equal power to painter and to poet
> Of daring all hath still been given: we know it.

---

1.   Swinburne - "A Study of Ben Jonson, 111-112.

Robert Herrick, 1591 - 1674.

Herrick, as one of the Cavalier Poets, was somewhat influenced by Horace's love poems, but that he was thoroughly acquainted with all of Horace's works is very apparent.
[1]
F.W.Moorman says that "while echoes from classical authors abound in Herrick's works, still Horace was his first love."

Herrick was so thoroughly acquainted with his Horace, that although he did not do much formal translation, he scattered many Horatian references and quotations throughout his poetry.

References and Quotations.

"To the Earl of Westmoreland."

"Virtue concealed with Horace you'll confess
Differs not much from drowsy slothfulness."

O. IV, 9, 29.

"paulum sepultae distat inertiae."

Hesperides -

"And once more yet ere I am laid out dead
Knock at a star with my exalted head."

Odes I, 1, 36.

"Sublimi feriam sidera vertice."

---

1. Robert Herrick - A Biographical and Critical Study, 216 sqq.

In "A Country Life to Thomas Herrick", he echoes many
of the sentiments of Horace,-some places are practically trans-
lations.

> "Thrice and above blest, my soul's half, art thou,
>
> In thy both last and better vow;
>
> Could'st leave the city for exchange to see
>
> The country's sweet simplicity."

While not an exact translation, comes very near to

> Epode, II, 1, 4.

> "Beatus ille qui procul negotiis,
>
> at prisca gens mortalium,
>
> paterna rura bobus exercet suis."

Again in the same poem he actually translates

O. I, 3, 9-12.

> "Illi robur et aes triplex
>
> Circa pectus erat qui fragilem truci
>
> commisit pelago ratem
>
> primus."

> "A heart thrice walled with oak and brass that man
>
> Had, first durst plough the ocean."

Herrick was perhaps not so much influenced in his love
poems by Horace as by Catullus and Anacreon but for his graver
poems, he looks to Horace for inspiration.   The poem entitled

"His Age" is clearly influenced by O. II, 14.

       "Eheu fugaces, Postume - etc."

and by   "Diffugere nives", O. IV, 7.

       "Ah, Poshumus! Our yeares hence flye,

      And leave no sound; nor piety,

         Of prayers, or vow

      Can keep the wrinkle from the brow:

         But we must on,

      As fate does lead or draw us; none,

      None, Poshumus, co'd ere decline

      The doom of cruell Proserpine.

      The pleasing wife, the house, the ground,

      Must all be left, no one plant found

         To follow thee,

      Save only the Curst-Cipress tree:"

The entire poem shows a philosophy more like the blend of Stoicism and Epicureanism found in Horace than a real Christian philosophy.

    Like Horace, also, Herrick felt that his work was to be ever lasting. Though many of the poets of the Renaissance had this same belief, Herrick seemed to cling to it more firmly than any of the others. We recall the poem with which Horace closed his third book of Odes, "Exegi monumentum aere perennius,"

and compare with it, two poems of Herrick's

"Upon Himself."

"Thou shalt not All die; for while Love's fire shines

Upon his Altar, men shall read thy lines;

And learn'd Musicians shall to honour Herrick's

Fame, and his Name, both set, and sing his Lyricks."

Also "His Poetry and his Pillar".

"Behold this living stone

I rear for me,

Ne'er to be thrown

Down, envious Time by thee.

"Pillars let some set up

If so they please

Here is my hope

And my Pyramides."

———————

John Milton, 1608 - 1674.

Milton was so fairly steeped in Classics that the
fact that he knew his Horace goes without saying.   That he
admired him and counted him among the great poets is clearly
shown in the following quotation from "On Education".

"I mean not here the prosody of verse ---- but that
sublime art which in Aristotle's poetics as in Horace and
others teaches what the laws of a true epic poem are, what of
a dramatic, what of a lyric, what decorum is, which is the
grand masterpiece to observe."

Milton translated one ode of Horace, but there are
innumerable passages throughout his works, which find a parallel
in Horace.

P.L. II, 554.   "How long or short permit to heaven."

Odes I, 12, 9.   "permitte divis cetera."

     Comus 96, "glowing axle."

     Odes I, i, 4. "fervidis rotis."

     Odes I, 2, 1. "dirae grandinis."

     P.L. II, 586. "dire hail."

     O. I, 2, 3. "iaculatus."

     P.L. VI, 665. "hurled to and fro with jaculation dire."

     O.I, 2, 34. "quam Iocus circum volat et Cupido."

L.A. 26. "Haste thee Nymph and bring with thee
jest and youthful jollity."

O.I, 2, 2. "rubente dextera."

Milton has "red right hand."

John Dryden, 1631 - 1700.

Dryden translated some of Horace's works and also imitated many of his poems, particularly the Satires.

In the preface to his translations, Dryden says of Horace:-

"That which will distinguish his style from all other poets is the numerousness of his verse.   There is nothing so delicately turned in all the Roman language.   There appears in every part of his diction --- a kind of noble purity. His words are chosen with as much exactness as Vergil's, but there is a greater spirit in them.   But the most distinguishing part of all his character seems to be his jollity and his good humor."

Dryden's translation of Ode III, 29, is famous; it has been said to be the one poem written in translation superior to the original on which it was founded.

"Descended of an ancient line
That long the Tuscan scepter swayed,

Make haste to meet the generous wine,

 Whose piercing is for thee delayed:

 The rosy wreath is ready made,

And artful hands prepare

The fragrant Syrian oil that shall perfume thy hair.

"When the wine sparkles from afar,

 And the well-natured friend crys, "Come away!"

Make haste, and leave they business and thy care;

No mortal interest can be worth thy stay.

Leave for a while thy costly country seat,

And to be great indeed, forget

Thy nauseous pleasures of the great.

"Make haste and come!

 Come and forsake thy cloying store!

 Thy turret that surveys from high

 The smoke, and wealth, and noise of Rome,

 And all the busy pagrantry

 That wise men scorn and fools adore.

 Come, give thy soul a loose, and taste the

 pleasures of the poor!

— — — — — — — — — — — — — — — — — —

"Happy the man, and happy he alone

 He who can call today his own;

 He who, secure within, can say,

———————

Tomorrow do thy worst, for I have lived today!

    Be fair or foul or rain or shine,

The joys I have possessed, in spite of Fate, are mine.

Not heaven itself upon the past has power,

And what has been, has been, and I have had my hour.

"Fortune that, with malicious joy,

    Does man, her slave, oppress,

Proud of her office to destroy,

    Is seldom pleased to bless;

Still various, and unconstant still,

But with an inclination to be ill,

Promotes, degrades, delights in strife,

And makes a lottery of life.

    I can enjoy her while she's kind;

    But when she dances in the wind,

And shakes the wings, and will not stay,

I puff the prostitute away.

    The little or the much she gave is quietly resigned;

Content with poverty, my soul I arm,

And virtue, though in rags, will keep me warm.

    "What is't to me,

Who never in her unfaithful sea,

If storms arise and clouds grow black

———————

If the mast split and threaten wreck?
Then let the greedy merchant fear
        For his ill gotten gain,
And pray to gods, that will not hear.
While the debating winds and billows bear
        His wealth into the main.
For me, secure from fortune's blows,
Secure of what I cannot lose,
In my small pinnacle I can sail,
        Contemning all the blustering roar;
And, running with a merry gale,
With friendly stars my safety seek
Within some little winding creek,
        And see the storm ashore."

23

Alexander Pope, 1688- 1744.

Pope used Horace's works very extensively, particularly The Satires.   In 1748, he published "Imitations of Horace" which Stemplinger tells us created as great a sensation as later Byron's Satirical Imitation of Ars Poetica.

His admiration of Horace is fully expressed in his "Essay on Criticism."

"Horace still charms with graceful negligence
And without method charms us into sense:
Will like a friend familiarly convey
The truest notions in the easiest way.
He, who supreme in judgment, as in wit,
Might boldly censure, as he boldly writ
Yet judged with coolness, tho he sung with fire
His precepts teach but what his works inspire."

In the Temple of Fame."

"There happy Horace tun'd th' Ausonian lyre
To sweeter sounds and tempered Pindar's fire.
Please with Alcaeus' manly rage t' infuse
The softer spirit of the Sapphic Muse."

Pope has many passages taken directly from Horace.
Essay on Crit. 268.

"Be Homer's works your study and delight,
Read them by day and meditate by night."

24

A.P. 268.

>"Vos exemplaria graeca

>Nocturna versate manu, versate diurna."

Essay on Crit.215.

>"A little learning is a dangerous thing

>Drink deep or taste not the Pierian Spring."

A.P. 372.

>"mediocribus esse poetis

>Non homines, no di, non concessere columnae."

Pope translated or rather imitated the Satires of Horace, but while evidently using certain Satires as patterns, he succeeded in writing something distinctly English, entirely his own, in style, subject matter and spirit.   To quote R.J.E.Tiddy in his lecture "Satire and Satura", "Horace's influence tempered the venom of Pope; or perhaps it would be fairer to say that Horace's satire was a mould into which Pope could pour his kindlier feelings.   But for all his miraculous ingenuity in adapting Horace to his own needs, Pope gives us something very different from Horace. He adds to him a vigour and a point that are Pope's."

[1]

In the introduction to Sat. II, 1. the editor says of Pope - "As a poet he had little in common (with Horace) besides a comprehensive knowledge of life and manners, and a certain curious felicity of expression -------- Nor was his temper

----

1. London Edition of Pope's Works.

less unlike that of Horace than his talents.   What Horace would
only smile at Mr. Pope would treat with the great severity
of a Persius: and what Mr. Pope would strike with the caustic
lightning of a Juvenal, Horace would content himself with turn-
ing into ridicule."

William Wordsworth - 1770 - 1850.

In a letter to Walter Savage Landor (1822) Wordsworth
makes this statement.   "My acquaintance with Virgil, Horace,
Lucretius and Catullus is intimate."

In Memoirs of Wordsworth II, 479, Bishop Wordsworth
tells us that the poet said "Horace is my great favorite, I
love him dearly."

"Musings near Aquapendente" 256 sqq.

>   "Or Sabine Vales inspire a wish
>   To meet the shade of Horace by the side
>   Of his Bandusian Fount."

"Those Breathing" 92.

>   "That life ------ which Horace needed for his
>   spirit's health;
>   Sighed for, in heart and genius overcome.
>   By noise and strife and questions wearisome
>   And the vain splendours of imperial Rome."

"Liberty" ll. 100 sqq.   Speaking of Horace -

>   "Give me the humblest note of those sad strains
>   Drawn forth by pressure of his gilded chains,

26

As a chance sunbeam from his memory fell

Upon the Sabine farm he loved so well,

Or when the prattle of Bandusia's spring

Haunted his ear, he only listening

He proud to please, above all rivals, fit

To win the palm of gaiety and wit;

He, doubt not, with involuntary dread,

Shrinking from each new favor to be shed,

By the world's Ruler, on his honored head."

These passages and many others, show a deep sympathy and understanding of Horace, that could have been gained only through constant companionship with his works.   This companionship also shows itself throughout Wordsworth's poems in chance quotations, and similarities of thought and wording.

To Scott embarking for Naples ▼

"Be true ye winds of the ocean and the midland sea

Wafting your charge to soft Parthenope."

op. I, 3, 3 sqq.

"Ventorumque regat pater

obstrictis aliis praeter Iapyga

navis, quae tibi creditum

debes Vergilium."

Invocation in "Ode to Duty."

"Stern Daughter of the Voice of God."

27

Ode I, 35.

"O diva, gradum quae regis Antium."

Of his Ode to Duty, Wordsworth says: "This Ode is on
the model of Gray's Ode to Adversity, which is copied from
Horace!s Ode to Fortune. (I. 35)

"Stanzas Composed in Simplon Pass." l. 8.

"Anio's precipitous flood."

cp. I, 7, 13.

"praeceps Anio."

Sonnet "Young England" 10-11

'An imitative race,

The servum pecus of a Gallic breed."

Cp. Epist. I, 19, 19. "o imitatores, serorum pecus."

"An Evening Walk" ll. 72 - 77.

Did Sabine grace adorn my living line ,

Bandusia's praise, wild stream, should yield to thine!

Never shall ruthless minister of death

Mid thy soft glooms the glittering steel unsheath;

No goblets shall, for thee, be crowned with flowers,

No kid with piteous outcry thrill thy bowers.

Cp. O. III, 13.

"O fons Bandusiae, splendidior vitro,

dulci digne mero non sine floribus,

cras donaberis haedo,

cui frons turgida cornibus

primis et venerem et proelia destinat;
frustra; nam gelidos inficiet tibi
   rubro sanguine rivos,
    lascivi suboles gregis."

Samuel Taylor Coleridge, 1772- 1834.

Coleridge evidently knew Horace, had studied him as a
boy at school, accepted him as one of the great poets, but was
less affected by him than most of the other poets of his age.

For his recognition of Horace's greatness see
"Lay Sermon".

"For this I refer you to the darling of the
polished court of Augustus, to the man whose works have been in
all ages deemed the models of good sense, and are still the
pocket companions of those who pride themselves on uniting
the scholar with the gentleman."

Coleridge also has traces of Horatian influence.
"Honour" 23-24.

"Or thunder at thy door the midnight train,

Or death shall knock that never knocks in vain."
Cp. Odes I, 4, 13.

"Pallida mors aequo pulsat pede pauperum tabernas."
"Easter Holidays" 13.

"With mirthful dance they beat the ground".

29

Cp. Ode I, 37, 1-2.

"Nunc pede libro

Pulsanda tellus."

From "On the Third Possible Church".

"Mons adhuc parturit; the ridiculus mus~~news~~ was but
an omen."

CP. A.P. 39. "parturient montes, nascetur ridiculus mus."

Motto of poem "To the Rev. George Coleridge".

"Notus in fratres animi paterni"

is a quotation of O. II, 2. 6.

"Talleyrand to Lord Grenville" 35-36.

"No time from my name this my motto shall sever,

'Twill be Non sine pulvere palma forever. "

Epist. I, 1, 51.

"Cui sit condicio dulcis sine pulvere palmae."

30

Lord Byron, 1788-1824.

Byron had conceived a great dislike for Horace in his
school days, because he was compelled to study his poems.   As
he says "I abhorred

> Too much to conquer for the Poet's sake
>
> The drilled dull lesson, forced down word by word
>
> In my repugnant youth."

Farther on in the same poem is the oft quoted line expressing
his dislike but the whole stanza really pays him tribute.

> "Then farewell Horace,- whom I hated so,
>
> Not for thy faults, but mine: it is a curse
>
> To understand, not feel thy lyric flow,
>
> To comprehend, but never love thy verse;
>
> Although no deeper moralist rehearse
>
> Our little life, nor Bard prescribe his art,
>
> Nor livelier Satirist the conscience pierce,
>
> Awakening without wounding the touched heart,
>
> Yet fare thee well - upon Soracte's ridge we part."

So, we see, Byron knew his Horace very well, and
scattered quotations throughout his works, but he did not fully
appreciate him.   In "Don Juan" 14, 77, he calls Horace
"The great little poet."   However, he took great pride in
his "Hints from Horace" a paraphrase of Ars Poetica.   Ten
years later in a letter to Murray he says, "I look upon it

31

(Hints from Horace) and my Pulci as by far the best things of
my doing."

The motto for his "Hints from Horace is taken from
Ars Poetica 304-5.

> "Ergo fungar vice cotis, acutum
> Reddere quae ferrum valet, exsors ipsa secandi."

Motto of a poem addressed to Edward Noel Long.

> "Nil ego contulerim iucundo sanus amico."

Cp. Sat. I, 5, 44.

On the title page of "Hours of Idleness."

> "Virginibus puerisque canto."

> Horace.

Cp.Ode III, 1, 4.

Don Juan I, 216.

> "My days of love are over; me no more
> The charms of maid, wife and still less of widow,
> Can make the fool of which they made before,-
> In short, I must not lead the life I do;
> The credulous hope of mutual minds is o'er,
> The copious use of claret is forbid too."

Byron adds this footnote.

> "Me nec femina nec puer
> Iam nec spes animi credula mutui,
> Nec certare iuvat miro
> Nec vincire novis tempora floribus."

32

Percy Bysshe Shelley, 1792-1822.

Shelley was more influenced by Horace than Byron, on account of his poetic love and appreciation of lyric expression; but he was essentially Greek in his tastes and so cared less for Horace.   In a letter to Thomas Peacock, Shelley says, "I had rather err with Plato than be right with Horace."   However, that he gave Horace high rank in literature is shown in his "Defense of Poetry."

"Let us assume that Homer was a drunkard, that Virgil was a flatterer, that Horace was a coward ...... Posterity has done ample justice to the great names now referred to."

In a letter to Hogg, he quotes

"Aliquando bonus dormitat Homerus."

Cp. A.P. 359.

Queen Mab.

"Slow necessity of death."

Cp. Odes I, 3, 32.

"tarda necessitas leti."

In a fragment, he has

"With triple brass

If calm endurance my weak breast I armed."

Cp. O. I, 3, 9-10.

"Aes triplex,

Circa pectus erat."

33

John Keats, 1795 - 1821.

[1] Keats was probably the least influenced by Horace of the English poets, there are only a few phrases which can be traced, and these are unimportant. He evidently had read at least a part of Horace for in a letter to John Hamilton Reynolds, he says,

"If I were well enough, I would paraphrase an ode of Horace's for you, on your embarking, in the seventy years ago style."

The reference is to Ode I, 3. To Virgil setting out for Greece.

Keats also consciously endeavored to avoid foreign influence. To his brother, he wrote:

"I shall never become attached to a foreign idiom so as to put it into my writings."

Alfred Tennyson, 1809-1892.

Tennyson was without a doubt, one of the poets most influenced by Horace. [2] Wilfred P. Mustard gives us innumerable

---

1. Mary Rebecca Thayer, "The Influence of Horace on the Chief
English Poets of the Nineteenth Century."

2. Wilfred P. Mustard,
"Classical Echoes in Tennyson."

quotations showing unmistakable Horatian influence, and yet
Tennyson himself says that he never appreciated Horace until
he was forty.   (Diary of William Allinghamp. 350.) He had
evidently like Byron been overdosed with Horace in his youth
but, to quote Mr. Mustard, "after the common experience of men,
his liking for the genial old Roman increased as the years went
by.   The first Latin he taught his own son was "O fons
Bandusiae."

Tennyson made up a metre, the Daisy, which he said was
a far off echo of the Horatian Alcaic.   In a note to his own
Alcaics, he says, "The Horatian Alcaic is the stateliest metre
in the world except the Virgilian hexameter at its best."

That Tennyson used Horace as a constant companion is
shown in Hallam Tennyson's Life of his father (II, 403) describ-
ing the journey to Italy.

"He took with him, his usual travelling companions,
Shakespeare, Milton, Homer, Virgil, Horace, Pindar, Theocritus,
and probably the Divina Comedia and Goethe's Gedichte."

In "Poets and their Bibliographics" 5.

"You, old popular Horace, you the wise adviser".
Epilogue to "The Charge of the Heavy Brigade" 46.

"For dare we dally with the spheres
As he did, half in jest,
Old Horace? I will strike said he
The stars with head sublime.

First part of poem "Will"

    "Oh well for him whose will is strong."

an echo of O. III, 3.

    "iustum et tenacem propositi virum."

Audley Court.

   "I woo'd a woman once,

   But she was sharper than an eastern wind."

O.I, 33, 15. "libertina fretis acrior Hadriae."

Princess -

   "The very nape of her white neck was rosed."

Odes I, 13, 2.

   "Cervicem roseam."

"A Dream of Fair Women". Cleopatra.

    "I died a Queen! The Roman soldier found

     Me lying dead, my crown upon my brows,

     A name forever! lying robed and crowned,

     Worthy a Roman spouse."

This Cleopatra is clearly the Cleopatra whom Horace describes as "generosius perire quaerens."

Odes I, 37, 30.

    "Scilicet invidens,

   privata diduci superbo

   non humilis mulier triumpho."

"The Vale of Bones" Tennyson uses

————————

36

"Your brows with noble dust defiled"

and quotes Horace's verse in a footnote 0. II, 1, 22.

"Non indecoro pulvere sordidos."

In Ulysses -   "When

Thro' scudding drifts the rainy Hyades

Vext the dim sea."

We find a parallel in 0. IV, 14, 20.

"In domitas prope qualis undas

exercet Auster, Pleiadum choro

scindente nubis, impiger hostium

vexare turmas."

William Makepeace Thackeray -1811-1863.

By some authorities, Thackeray is considered the most
Horatian of all English writers.   Both are satirists, Horace
writes in verse and Thackeray in prose, but the method and
spirit are similar, as well as the objects of their satire.
Both satirize the bore,- we call to mind the famous bore as
the Via Sacra of Sat. I, 9 and compare Thackeray's Talbot
Troysden.   Both satirize the snob.   We recall Nasidiemus
dinner party of Sat. II, 8.   The fourth epode also shows Horace's
contempt for the vulgar rich.

"Licet superbus ambules pecunia,

Fortuna non mutat genus.

Videsne, sacram metiente te viam

Cum bis trium alnarum toga,

37

Ut ora vertat huc et huc nuntium

    Liberima indignatio?"

Thackeray expresses the same thought in his portrayal
of the Osbornes, Lady Clavering, Coxe, Tuggeridge and others.

Both Thackeray and Horace believed in a gentle method
of Satire:

    "Ridiculum acri

Fortius et melius magnas plerumque secat res."
Says Horace Sat. I, 10, 14-15.

"To laugh at such is Mr. Punch's business. May he laugh
honestly, hit no foul blow, and tell the truth when at his
broadest grin ----- never forgetting that if Fun is good, Truth
is better, and Love is best of All."

Thackeray Book of Snobs, Conclusion.
Newcomes I, 38, 10.

"Black Care sits behind all sorts of horses and
gives a trinkgeld to postilions all over the map." is an obvious
parallel to Odes III, 1, 40.

    "Post equidem sedet atra cura."

38

Robert Browning, 1813-1889.

Robert Browning's father, it is said, knew by heart,
all of the odes of Horace, and the natural conclusion is that
he taught his son to love the poet to whom he was so deeply
attached.   Browning certainly quotes Horace very readily,
not only the more common and familiar passages, but those more
seldom quoted by others.   William Sharp, in his Life of Brown-
ing tells us that Browning began translating Horace at the age
of eight.   There are many traces of Horace in his works, but
not as many as we might expect from his deep knowledge of that
poet.   Miss Thayer accounts for this by the fact that Browning
was haturally self-concealing, that he lived in the character
he was portraying and so did not show his Classical knowledge
unless his character was one learned in Classical literature.

From Pacchiarotto, Stanza 16.

> "The paraphrase which I much need is
> From Horace - per ignes incedis."

Cp. O. II, 1, 7.

> "incedis per ignes."

The Ring and the Book, 9.

> "Quid vetat, what forbids, I aptly ask,
> With Horace."

Cp. Sat. I, 1, 25.

Fifine at the Fair, Stanza 82.

> "Try if, trusting to sea tracklessness I class
> With those around whose breast grew oak and triple brass;

———

39

Who dreaded no degree of death, but with dry eyes,

Surveyed the turgid main and its monstrosities,

And rendered futile so, the Prudent Power's decree

Of separate earth and dissociating sea;

Since, how it is observed, if impious vessels leap

Across, and tempt a thing they should not touch

    the deep?

Cp. Ode I, 3, 9 sqq.

    "Illi robur et aes triplex

       Circa pectus erat

    - - - - - - - - -

    Quem mortis timuit gradum,

       Qui siccis oculis monstra natantia

    Qui vidit mare turbidum.

    - - - - - - - - -

    Nequiquam deus abscidit

       Prudens Oceano dissociabili

    Terras, si tamen impiae

       Non tangenda rates transiliunt vada.

From a letter to Mr. Fox.

    "A free and easy thing he wrote some months ago

"on one leg."

Cp. Sat. I, 4, 9, 10.

       "In hora saepe ducentos,

      Ut magnum, versus dictabat stans pede uno."

40

Thus we see that Horace has been really a potent
influence in English Literature.   Possibly his greatest
influence, to quote Stemplinger, is the "general enriching
of lyric poetry." In many cases it is hard to trace, but
we somehow feel the spirit of Horace permeating whole works
of a writer, cropping out at unexpected places in spite of the
stronger force of the writer's own individuality.   This is
perhaps a natural result of the intensive study which the boys
in English schools make of Horace, but that he is essentially
human and appeals to the heart of every one who reads his works,
is I believe the real reason.   For, to quote,Frederick MacDonald

"Many an emancipated school boy who has said with
Byron, 'Then farewell Horace whom I hated so', has lived to find
as Byron did that Horace has fixed in the perfect expression of
his enduring verse thoughts which life inevitably suggest to
every man; and that lines once associated with the drudgery of
the schoolroom came to mind in after days with the aptness of
a proverb, the weight of an oracle, and the charm of a remembered
song. ------ The Odes of Horace have been dear to fifty genera-
tions of students, divines, and toilers in various fields."

BOOKS CONSULTED.

Edward Stemplinger: Das Fortleben der Horazischen Lyrik seit
              der Renaissance.

Hugo Reinsch: Jonson's Beziehungen zu Horaz" in Menchener,
              Beitrage zur romanishen und englishen Philologie.

Edward Moore: Studies in Dante.

Manitius: Horace and Dante.

R.G.Tucker: Foreign Debt to English Literature.

Skeat Edition of Chaucer.

C.G.Osgood: Concordance to Poems of E.Spenser.

H.R.D.Anders: Shakespeare's Books.

F.W.Moorman: Robt. Herrick, a biographical and critical Study.

Bradshaw: Concordance to Milton.

Sampson: Studies in Milton.

Dryden's Poems - Edinburgh Edition.

Works of Alexander Pope - London Edition.

Karl Kuchenbacher: Dryden as a Satirist.

R.J.E. Tiddy: Satire and Satura.

Mary R.Thayer: Influence of Horace on the Chief English Poets
              of the 19th Century.

Frederick W.MacDonald: Recreations of a Booklover.

G.M.Showerman: Horace and Thackeray.

APPROVED M. S. Slaughter

Professor of Latin

6/15/17

www.ingramcontent.com/pod-product-compliance
Lightning Source LLC
Chambersburg PA
CBHW052239290725
30338CB00008B/213